LIFE IN THE CANOPY

To Susan,

Thanks for sharing this time under the Canopy

Bon Rice
Stoen Sept 25/2004

LIFE IN THE CANOPY

BRUCE RICE

WITH PHOTOGRAPHS BY
CHERIE WESTMORELAND

HAGIOS PRESS
Box 33024 Cathedral PO
Regina SK,   S4T 7X2

Text copyright © 2009 Bruce Rice / Images copyright © 2009 Cherrie Westmoreland

Library and Archives Canada Cataloguing in Publication
Rice, Bruce
    Life in the canopy / by Bruce Rice.

Poems.
ISBN 978-1-926710-00-6

    I. Title.

PS8585.I128L54 2009   C811'.54   C2009-905139-7

Edited by Harold Rhenisch.
Cover Design by Tania Wolk, Go Giraffe Go Inc.
Cover Art "Fall Fire" by Cherie Westmoreland.
Typeset by Tania Wolk.
Printed at Friesen's Corperation, Altona, Manitoba.
Printed and bound in Canada.
Set in Gill Sans.

All rights reserved. No part of this book may be reproduced, stored in a retrieval system or transmitted in any form or by any means without the prior written permission of Hagios Press, except in the case of a reviewer, who may quote brief passages in a review. In the case of photocopying or other reprographic copying, users must obtain a license from Access Copyright, Toronto, Ontario.

Hagios Press gratefully acknowledges the support for the production of this book as provided by:

For more information on Hagios Press and our books: www.hagiospress.com

for Joanne, Keegan and Mira

CONTENTS

- 1 Drifters
- 4 Europe
- 6 Winter
- 9 The Question They Always Ask
- 12 Renovations
- 21 Freehouse Wasp
- 22 La Bodega
- 23 Wasp Memory
- 25 Crawlspace
- 27 Strange Little Poem
- 29 The Wind
- 35 The Regina School
- 37 Dear Bob, Your Smallpox Blanket
- 45 A New Manifesto
- 46 Flying Southeast
- 48 Festival
- 51 Dead Métis at Batoche
- 58 "Bruce" On Loan
- 62 The Same Light
- 63 Life in the Canopy
- 67 On a Clear Day You Can See Forever
- 69 Interview
- 71 Drum Village
- 73 Elsa's Argyle Street Serenade
- 75 Elsa's Dream
- 77 Coyote Willow
- 80 My So-Called Career
- 82 Heart
- 84 Me and Dad at the Regina Riot
- 89 Mira, With a Black Guitar
- 92 Regina Conservatory
- 93 Last Night
- 95 A Window
- 97 Walking
- 99 As He Left Me
- 101 Appetite
- 104 Flyway
- 105 Vacancy
- 106 Waskesiu
- 110 Not Zen But Close Enough
- 112 Inside the Quality Tea Room
- 118 Plough Winds
- 126 Saskatoon Berry
- 129 Swans

IMAGES *by Cherie Westmoreland*

8	North of Pilot Butte
36	Victoria Park, Regina
50	B-Say-Tah Point, Qu'Appelle Valley
60	East of Craven, Qu'Appelle Valley #1
60	East of Craven, Qu'Appelle Valley #2
61	East of Craven, Qu'Appelle Valley #3
79	Wakamow Valley, Moose Jaw
91	South of Avonlea
103	Valeport, Qu'Appelle Valley
109	Anglin Lake
125	Echo Lake, Qu'Appelle Valley
131	Near Earl Grey

DRIFTERS

Your school friends go home —
                                        leave you working past midnight.
    Everything's cool.

Clapton plays *Layla* on the stereo as your canvas fills
with the lifetimes of clouds —
                the vanishing point of everything you've learned so far.

                      I write until three and get up at six. We all do.
Aunt Jessie painted only at night and finally eloped
with the elevator agent.
                Uncle Hugh
designed carpets that sold all over Europe.
He never slept either.
              His uncle was a builder of bridges.

My great-grandfather's father broke horses and drowned in the Hudson,
        and if I think about it long enough I'll know the whole story.

Over the years we've come to inhabit a continent.
         Tracks run into the blue everywhere we look.
                       We pace and we walk,
drift with a feeling for currents as slow-moving ships crawl through the night.

                   The house never sleeps. Your hands
       work by themselves and the room
shines as if a bell has been touched. This is the moment; you know there is more.

           The stones by the sea
where we strolled last summer are the same stones my grandfather walked
on his way to the jute mill. He was twelve
and he worked the hackler.

              The sepia wash on the canvas stretched on the table
is the Tay where he clung to a footing, his skiff dipping low in the whirlpool,
his pals on shore,

      tide coming in.

This prairie we live in could be veldt, these rising fields,
the way that we always go back to the sea.
                              What I say now
could be what my father wrote at seventeen:
                                        dust, dust, and dust again.

What you do here is harder to come by. These hours you love
owe you nothing.

                    The brush touches down
in a thalo blue swirl,
            your sense of the surface.

You paint yourself into a landscape — barely a stroke;
                    a figure looks back for the sake of the road.

EUROPE

Children are starving in Europe, my father
used to say as he glowered
at the watery heaps
of minced meat spooned to the sides
of our plates. Of course, we were kids
and couldn't imagine what he meant, the dead
smoldering beneath the ground he walked each day.
Out of the blue my brother
piped up, *Why don't we mail it to them then?*
It was one of those moments
in a difficult time. My father
spat his tea onto his plate as he laughed,
which made us howl all the harder. At last,
something dim and close to the ground was gone from the house.

I do the cooking now but my children don't come home,
so I sit in front of the TV, fuming and depressed. It's all about
waste and what we consume each day without desire,
in silence, and the fact that desire is wasted.

The news drones on.
It seems an unworthy thing if no one dies, if
five hundred thirsty
vessels wrapped in rags do not totter,
resigned and anemic in the ditch
as armour filmed from a low angle roars by: gasoline and death.

We march in the park,
carry our children, burn candles and sing
or pray or weep all night.
The longer it goes on the more we hunger.
We despair that the right thing will never
be allowed, that the real thing is the real thing.
And it does not change.

Whatever I do is never enough.
I will never earn my father's wound.
The news comes on and they say
the waters of the world are rising.
Famine in every country.

WINTER

                              January gone,
the weight of winter has missed us,
                                    muscles ease,
and the year before runs into this one:
                                      there'll be no brittle tapping of branches.
The weather tells us everything.
                      The third year
of open water on the lake.
          Solitary summer birds climb
higher in the trees, their colours drained
among dead leaves and the racket
                          of raiding sparrows.

                    The cold
that pushed us to the edge of what one must endure
may never come,
           everything's forgotten,
                        our battered texts no longer teach

          The glittering roofs are still with frost; each worn
          Black chimney builds into the quiet sky…

Nothing to attach a memory to — no warning twinge of frostbite,
black blood burning in my fingertips
                              as I ran the long way home, ran
though I was told not to run. That kind of cold will burst a lung's small atmosphere.
I learned to vanish like a partridge in a drift, close my eyes,
                                             lashes white,
             beneath the season's edge.

On film days at Arthur Peachy School
I watched our Arctic stuttering,
                        old scars jumping on a snowy screen;
harpoon in hand,
              I stalked the sea's dark rim,
                                   looking back,
impossible to imagine the white bear that walks upside-down under ice,
underneath its own reflection, could drown.

             All those years I lived beside my enemy, the cold,
but this warm weather knows me less. There is nothing here to fear or love.
They say the further north you go
                          the worse it gets.
Waxwings sing above the yaw, earth heaves
                                beneath the drying walk;
something deep is vaguely grieving.

THE QUESTION THEY ALWAYS ASK

                                           Why Regina?
Why anywhere?
                 Because a sandy-haired woman
                                  selling tickets
remembered my poem in a book she bought for a dollar and now she's my wife.

I couldn't find work, so my dad loaned me his antique Royal Underwood; it weighed
       14 pounds and I mostly recall those first delirious poems for the way
the roller clacked and racket they made.

                                But that's not a reason. It wasn't my town
and driving south one evening just to get out I rolled to a stop by a coulee;
       eight antelope raced soundlessly into a shadow where they disappeared.
I stood by the road and watched as the prairie returned to shortgrass and light
                                        as if I'd seen nothing at all.

I canoed in a creek — a narrow ribbon of water the colour of old bronze,
barely a scratch on floor of the valley as it slipped under fields
                           where blackbirds got drunk
on fermented choke cherries and fell to the ground.

The magic hour filled the line of purple hills to the brim.
I drifted round a bend
     as the bough of a willow arched over the water,
reached into its own reflection
and in that reflection
      seven motionless herons.

It seems more and more places put a mortgage on everything, prices go up;
roots get tangled with other roots, and you can't up
           and leave in any old storm.
Now friends I met here have died and I think how the trees in these parts
live to a human age;
     they're more frail than they look and dark, and their visage
speaks to the part of you that doesn't want consoling.

My kids are more of these streets than they know.
They tell me they've forgotten nights on the porch wrapped in quilts
as the moon in eclipse
                        hangs like an orange over the yard.
One night they'll lift their own children to see the same close moon,
                           play the same taste-game,
feel small fingers grip through the blanket's fold and wonder why
they thought of that,
                 just then.

                      There are no mountains here,
                        nor harbours;
all you see is an urban lake, a hundred thousand trees in the forest we planted.
          You come to a place and either you see it or you don't
and if you do it means you've taken it into yourself.
As for love, it's hard, here too —
        open-ended with a hundred resolves,
then it keeps changing
and no one can say: *Why this place, why anywhere?*

RENOVATIONS

A house remembers everything — wooden-handled hammers aimed
                at their shadow or hooked on the trusses of a darkening sky: *1913*,
           a double-hinged banging
as the westering wind gusts through the open roof. I knock down
lath, smash white blocks cast as plaster dripped
to the foot of the studs,
                    then I regret it.

Raw fir bristles with splinters, timber
pulls tight to itself like an age of bone
and I wear out a drill and sander on the same night:
                studs at sixteen-inch centers
and three nails in every joint. One year after the cyclone,
the carpenter swore: *This one. This one will stand.*

It remembers the tough years: *Adam Little Blacksmith,*
the Hungarian boarder hired to shoe and exercise horses in the Germantown livery
while farmhands slept it off, sprawled
like pieces of wood tossed on the floor of the loft
                            two bits a night, no questions asked.

And still more creaking and dreaming: *Potatoes and minced meat*
boiling in the kitchen. Elsie Cameron, the skinny Scottish cook
burns everything. Just one spice: salt — but no one
complains since she's just as happy to throw you out.

Dwelling: excavating down to roots and small bones,
                into everything fading or gone,
           wolves with grasslines still green in their eyes;
                        a whistle — a hawk bone,
    a hollowed-out cry.

1924 — the Taylor twins laid out on the table,
                                  perfect and cool
        as pieces of porcelain. Reverend Rees jolts upright mid-Psalm.
The boy's chest starts to *rise*, his eyes flip open, taking it in,
                                in silence.
How brief and blue hope is.

Here's a strange one: Mike and Maggie blind drunk.
Maggie gets up one morning to light the stove,
staggers around banging the lids
                                and dropping the lifter.
Mike charges in with a roar,
                              grabs the skillet with both hands;
a blow to the head and he kills her. *Your Honour*, he says,
wiping his eyes, *I just couldn't take*
                            the god damned racket.

The room with the knee-wall.

Like eddies nibbling a sand spit in the smooth part of the river,
                whispers
                              swirl in the red of the wood
a murmur,
        delicious
                          a slap
                                a caress
as love shows up like a bed in a landscape
a creak and a gap
        a creak
                and a gap.

❧

I'm working on floors at midnight again. Sixty-mill grit. The sander's a lumbering thing
that wants to veer off like an overweight twin. Vibrations plunder my bones,
                     and can't be shut off.
            The house is its own.

※

Like young men off to a war, the forests are gone; this wood will never be again.
I run my fingers over the surface made smooth at last and recall
           my father, how he loved true things.
If he were here he might recall one more thing: hoarfrost
shrouding the tree outside his one-room school, bejeweling
the weathervane, which was made of course
by Adam Little (very little), blacksmith,
      who fell in love with the teacher.

Four Septembers ago, my father's tales went AWOL, not wanting to report.
         They've slipped between cracks or lie where they drifted.
   No space is ever empty.

※

I can't stop looking at the skin of the wood. The chorus
of tongues can't stop clacking. I'm on my knees, tapping
and listening for the rapport of joists under the floor,
getting closer.
Worklight
spills sideways across the grain, like dawn,
tongue to groove, everything right, the way it was
when it first fit together: less like a conversation, and more like understanding.

I start in the closet, set down the can of stain. Boards want to speak
and their color rises, rhetorical, like when it was still in the tree.

The stain sets quickly. Bumps left by the dust have voices like fingerprints.
It's only fir after all,
meant to be covered, to rise two stories hidden in walls,
balloon frames shooting twenty-eight feet to the attic, circular tattoos
burned into the wood where the spinning saw wobbled and screamed
as the log fed through the mill.

I am followed
    by sun through the new windows of the dreamt-of library,
        by songs of birds,

  the ones that fly east from mountains in winter,
          notes
       trailing off before they are seen.

The branch outside the window springs and I hear a flutter.
The room is empty and listening,
    a hum beyond hearing: until the gaps are caulked, the desk
pushed back to the wall: the books and shelves of brick-a-brack, a Chinese box,
a wash of voices clambering for order,
      theirs and mine.

The neighbor's light snuffs out on the east wall, a moonless night
                      caught between houses. Icicles wink,
                                                          stitch parcels of dark.
            No one sees them fall but you hear them shatter.

There used to be words for the way it is now like calico, deep enough
for everything.
                          Imagine a delta, a riverhead
        where fiery blue flowers are borne on the current,
some on the water and some in the sky,
                                  a glimmer that flows under bridges
and goes on to the sea.

These days I'm followed by language and I love how it comes up the walk:
        caulk and chalk and brass lock, the future waiting to be appended.
Ninety-four years. I wonder how long this place will stand: all those years of nights,
the family din and the slow steps of our intentions.

                It will never be finished: the shape of what we begin.

                Each sigh
is a half-finished room.

FREEHOUSE WASP

We're all Presbyterians here. The earnest
                              Wheat Pool building
wears the blue-gray prairie air like chain mail at four in the afternoon.
In a week the moon will tumble into dust.
Swans will sweep wingtip to wingtip above the thing we buried like a stone.

A woman's agile voice rises from the deck.
                                       Passport laughter.
The waiter doesn't judge. This is not the first poem he's been in
and it's too soon to count tips or interrupt this reverie with questions
about salad, so he leaves the scribbler alone.

Try to imagine
                an afternoon
where everyone gets served and has, as they say, a life. And let's agree
that soon this summer will be gone and we will mourn
                          the disarray of glasses, the beer rings
drying on the table and the reedy tune in the speaker.

No one sees the silent blaze,
                          a small dark star in a country of towers.
The peregrine hunts between the high new steel — a flash, then gone.
Death is just a bump in the conversation
                                at four in the afternoon

LA BODEGA

The smoker sent outdoors by his addiction finds
his shaken system warmed,
everything decoded. The sidewalk
heaves with whatever sigh winter left behind.
The hatch of brownish moths drag themselves up trunks of haggard trees.
It is the age of calculation. *When to buy?*
Where to put the palms and potted plants? Here, perhaps —
somewhere near these sporty college kids, who now
decant their high school loves, a grade ten class where everything's
a dance and a disaster.

A reggae tune squeezing through a shoe-box speaker
circles the deck like an exotic talking bird that doesn't want
to leave its bungalow. It lifts its emerald throat
into the evening and everything's reduced to waves. Earth and the dying sun
get on with it. For now this island is; the sea has no name.
                                        On deck,
the aimless smokers wonder where they are, slightly giddy
with the hum they cannot place, the sudden chill —
smiling as they bend into their cigarettes.

WASP MEMORY

I am surprised how many are left
                    warning the air,
                                        tracers whizzing
            past my face as their busted-up home
blows away like eyelashes.

                    They stung me weeks ago and now
I caulk everything that's hollow,
                the holdouts they inhabit
as they shed their cowls.
                                        History
                    after all's
        a crevice memory.

The thought of them comes at me.
I envy them their boundaries,
                                the way they build again,
            generous in ways the world is not.

I do not move and still
                          they know me.
          I arrive like all explorers,
                                the malevolent shade in a dream,

                                        the ruin to follow.

CRAWLSPACE

This is the place for the howl of a cat,
                where the moon does not sing.

                              I live
on my belly — 'til the world drags me out.
Bed springs stab the dirt: Was this my fierce slumber?

Each time I inch my way out to the world,
                    turn at the opening and drop
to the floor in a shroud of silt, it gets
           harder to be where I am.

Having come to the end of the island, I go
                              no further,
    a dim half-thing of the bestiary with ferrous eyes,

                        a trick of the light at the edge of the jungle,
the way our gaze meets —
            the distance between us, harder to cross
than the low place in a human cave

            before it opens like language, wild
or spoken,
                        as it traps

and frees us at the same time.

STRANGE LITTLE POEM

It happens to us all, the thirty poems I lost last week
turned to scrolls of Farsi — which apparently,
my computer speaks. A hundred times a day a life's work
disappears, burned by an ill-tempered spouse,
the unstrung corpse of a lower case tribute
to e. e. cummings
slumped among the bags at the bottom of a dumpster.

I was almost relieved at what I could not do myself
(trash them all). I'll get a poem from this, I thought,
but not the usual allusion to how all the things that once existed
still exist — they're merely tanning on a beach
somewhere in the ether.
That poem never came, thank Christ.
The very idea of it, I thought, be damned.

But trying not to listen
gave me pause: strange word, "ether," the name
we had before the thing itself was found. Like "atoms,"
or a child's footprint as she skipped a million years ago through ash,
just before the rain, and just like atoms: proof
                    we knew the world hummed
before we had the walking-word for "song;"
before we left the plain.

THE WIND *Regina Cyclone, June 30, 1912*

1.

No one knows where it comes from.

              Walls have no time
before they are cloven. We're
driven into ourselves, picked up
and set down clutching the last thing we held —
as if it mattered.

28 dead, 31 dead.
      Who really knows?
The cupola of the new Baptist church
rolls down the street, Hallelujah.

2.

And here is its calling card.
A fringe of black. A turquoise sky
swirls — moves into town. The card's
been presented: five hundred
houses fly up, shuffled like shingles. Rail cars vanish;
the train can't be found. Smith Street shorn
straight up the middle. A bust-up,
a miracle. Sixty shop girls stare out the side
of the Y.W.C.A.

3.

It circles us all: the city
unbuilt. Roots and anchors:
our shelves rearranged.

A policeman says the ringing is only
inside our ears. Then sheets of rock
sliding: we know it by now.
A warehouse collapses. Running:
who's gone? Names and the whimpers of sifting dust.

4.

Disconsolate twilight.

We'll come back tomorrow to grope through the caves
                                    of our homes.
Doctors shout, *Lift up that lamp, God dammit,*
as the dark moans around them.
All over Germantown they hear it too,
a kind of half-sob, the way
a prisoner weeps without dreaming.

5.

What we know now is
the century begins,
but nobody owns it. Sun shines
on ignorant beasts.
Dogs bark. Horses toss their manes
to shake off the flies. And the wind —
the wind is already in us,
the wave that advances up mountains:
both ocean and fire, the tolling
of bells before they're torn free.

Breeze cools a field
and there's no harm in it. We see: an English
gentleman, the pleasant tapping
of grasses and his unnamed
melancholia. Wind stiffens the waves
and he almost forgets it, later,
writes, "Daffodils."

THE REGINA SCHOOL

We cling to anything that shines
in this new prairie town. One century done,
we know nothing of architecture
                                              and do not love
the Chicago School in search of an American form
or Frank Lloyd Wright's
                            epiphany, the bungalow,
though there are many here in prosperous *subdivisions*:
funny word that — for what can be below divisions? That which
cannot be parted.
                        Memory perhaps, or air.

All we have is post and beam. No Ionic
pillar in our speech.
In less than twenty years the righteousness
has emptied out of us. Thanks to our utilitarian, socialist ways
in this out-of-the way province,
we believe in nothing but what we can see,
VLTs and big box stores. Which is to say
we believe in nothing.

As I say: post and beam.
Every curve is precious, the sine wave of the Sask Power Building
or the gathering-in of Credit Union Central, monument
to our earthy cooperative past. Now everything's
post-something.
                      I long for the serif, the human
touch of how we build and what we read:
                                  half an arch,
something for the spirit to pass through, not as difficult
as the eye of a needle but still requiring
our belief and our attention.

DEAR BOB, YOUR SMALLPOX BLANKET

                        hangs in Committee Room 1, and when
the meeting carries on for hours
because someone doesn't want "those people"
in their back yard, I think
you planned this all along,
sending those blankets back
to where they came from.

They're only painted circles:
                                  blue for spirit
rose for what the flesh endures —
not so far from what we wear now.

                         And it is strange magic,
                the way we're made of maps,
photographs from a hundred miles up
of wartime houses, arterials and grids —
a municipal diction: the CPR main line
cutting the town in half as if someone
dragged a sabre on the ground.
Pull back further and we disappear
into the plain, the dry canals and
craters, and the dim haze
of something burning.

                              Thirty neighbourhoods,
a hundred and thirty-three subdivisions: name a thing
and that's what it becomes, like
Hillsdale, so named after Fred Hill,
though no one thinks of the aging
scion feeding the boomtime need:
a memory now. His sons
look south from twin glass towers sunk
into the earth and the creaking bones of history.

❧

Wash Acres: sounds like wall-shakers,
for clapboard bungalows thrown up in a field
when the Mounties weren't looking. Or Wascana:
Cree name for the creek that
seeps from the marsh this side of Riceton,
meandering southeast to northwest—
a crooked arrow through the heart of the city — then dropping
though coulees as light-stepping coyotes
skip and touch their noses to the ground.
White-belled hop flowers ladder the bank
and grow up into the trees. Carp nudge the wall
               of the PFRA dam downstream,
then it continues into the Qu'Appelle, flowing
east, *Kisisakatchewani*, past silent pipestone quarries,
into the Assiniboia River —   a ribbon crossing
the black-earth bed of old Lake Agassi, meeting the Red
then splitting north to Lake Winnipeg
or south to the Mississippi,
past Natchez and Choctaw homelands
      into the world's water,
                           into the Gulf.

                         White-tailed deer and the occasional moose
follow the creek into town, lured by a feast
of fat, watered grass and fences
propping up boughs — a burden of apples.
The name, Wascana, these days, has been taken
over by cul-de-sacs: Wascana View, Wascana Heights,
Wascana East. No one knows how
they all appeared with double garages,
RVs and barbecues,
                              their greenways
and artificial lakes repeated like pixels.
It's nice the kids say, but it's easy to get lost.
                              Each row of houses
pushes back grain fields — not a true wilderness,
just one monoculture sliding over another.

We have big city dreams but it's like
going to a dance in your uncle's suit — sometimes it just
doesn't fit. It's easy to say "inner city" at meetings in Toronto
where ten thousand people
live on the street — just as many IV users
in East Vancouver, a place not much bigger
than here, but *MacLean's* says
It sells magazines.

If you wanted a poor man's map of Regina, you'd
start up a combine with a mile-wide swather
on the west side of town and keep driving
east for two miles until you hit MacDonalds:
stop for lunch and that would be your Stats Can map.

And Bob, it's funny how the names in that swath
would fall. Dieppe, McNab, North Central —
kids there call it "The Hood" after a movie no one
remembers. Lacking a story they know of
they've made it their own, like the Hills,
or it could mean it's nobody's home.
Now let's clip off a piece of Regent Park, not Toronto's
infamous flop now in rehab, but strictly
blue collar, then Coronation Park and North East,
where the Métis mow their lawns and gather
in school gyms under a banner — blue ribbon stitched
to a wavering sky.

           Then Glen Elm,
Eastview, and Core. There are no *Vistas* or
                        Lakes to *View* here: just immigrants,
Assiniboines, Nakota and Cree two generations off the reserve,
couch-surfing kids, seniors stuck between
neighbours who keep changing, drum circles and
Chinese apothecaries, the Ukrainian Coop, Oscar's Deli, a needle-strewn
art park, missing kids,
                    a casino,
the hallowed park of the Regina Riot and Manifesto over which swans
and geese safely migrate, the Serbian Church and the chickenwire run
in Jim Elliot's yard where he teaches snowy owls
to want to fly again, and the names beneath maps,
the ones we take into ourselves when we
want to make art in a way that has nothing
to do with someone else's mythology, and all we want to do is
                                    love the place that is here,
give it it's true name, and simply by refusing to leave
wrap ourselves in the thing that we are.

A NEW MANIFESTO

This is the Age of Plenty where fever
 has been — all the ghosts silenced.
I know them; they bind me:
 Let's hear no more.

No more of those who speak, having sat at the feet
 of prophets, in whose name they say The Masses
are hungry. Prophets have their speech.
 We have ours.

If we must have an anthem, let it be written
 for the instruments of doubt —   the music of failure.
Let nothing be done unless it's for Beauty; nothing must weigh so much
 that a child, who is five, with arms outstretched, cannot lift it.

Let us survey our griefs and love's tender indecencies
 and be judged by that measure. There'll be no turning back
for our losses, except that we know them.
 This is our means. The losses are ours.

We'll be fierce in conscription, as human life
 is conscripted. We know in our hearts
what must be abolished: the *Act* that undoes the grace of the other.
 We share one table; we name these ills.

FLYING SOUTHEAST

                     Flying southeast
from Regina, you see the place where God
gave up on agriculture: the land
packed with potholes (although we don't
like that word here) as though the Almighty
decided to take all the holes
in His stories, the place where one Book
or another sags or the text
isn't clear, moved them together,
and called it Saskatchewan.

But Life likes a hollow place.
Rain fills it up, then come the cattails,
mud hens, and foxes yipping
and scouting the shoregrass for nests
and things that stay motionless. Clouds skip
from one slough to another like a kind of Morse code.
September brushes the hilltops and rills, descends
as the coulees come into winter and a single
Balm of Gilead tree, a solitary giant,
lifts its scarred branches as patches of starlight
catch on the tips.

A few lonely farms throw their halos about them
and await a nativity scene. We already know
what it takes, what kind of people live there and why
they're so few.
It is clear by now this isn't
an allegory. It is simply the truth. Make of it
what you will.

REGINA FOLK FESTIVAL

> *African Combo $4.00*
> *Coke $2.00*

You wait in the breeze by a billowing door,
                cool as a porcelain sill.

There is no journey.
            No Tibet.

      It all comes down
               to a juggler's green flame.

                            These are dragonfly lands; they hatch
from the brim of the sinking sky.

We greet and let go with our eyes.
                My red guitar (drumming-on).

It's wrong to stop singing of love,
so applause for the golden light of our City Hall, applause

                              for the stars' blue isles
       and the ruby clouds beneath our feet.

I am shoeless and I come by the language of staving air.

                Feed me.

DEAD MÉTIS AT BATOCHE *Batoche, Sculpture in clay by Joe Fafard*

1.

Spare me your elegies
Give me a song

That rises like grass
A root that winter can't kill

Give me a language
Give me my skin

My feet
In a field of starlight that rises

Until either it's Earth
Or Heaven

The moon like a footlight
At the end of the road

2.

Everything breathes
You say you know

What you have
In your hands

This fumbling's proof
You're not ready

At seventeen years I buried my wife
Now here you come

Rubbing dirt in my eyes
And this girl plays a tune for a man

Nobody knows
Dust on the floor after the dance

The village asleep
As the church bell is stolen

3.

Where are my shoes
My shoes are out walking

(La-la-la on my grandchildren's tongues)
Getting lost and fitting

Anyone who tries them on
Me I don't worry

When my shoes come back
My feet will be gone

4.

There are no blackbirds here
The kind that sing at night

So poets say
Small things gone

As I am gone
Lost in the slurry

You say nothing's left you've done
What you came here to do

Take it from me
You will never finish

5.

My hand wants to reach
In my pocket

It can't understand
They've taken my pipe

A shadow remains
Where such things have been

A whetstone
A life

6.

I used to write to my love
Of the way her dress whispers

Grazing the ground
Her steps

In the willing grass
Indistinguishable from rain

They say she has gone
To some place in the earth

If I could speak
I could find her

7.

I feel your voice
As you feel mine

Death is a language
We both understand

Who is to say this word
Is eloquent or this one

Grievous
The hour calls

The dead cannot answer
The living can't hear it

Folding your coat on your arm
You give it no thought

A lament for the fallen
Drifting away

"BRUCE" ON LOAN *Joe Fafard Retrospective Exhibition*

There is the only one bull in this field.
Bruce the Black Aberdeen Angus
finds himself on the second floor
of the MacKenzie Gallery, set between
Vince Van Gogh (sprawled on the couch)
and Cezanne (whose restrained cypress trees
and blue mountain haze are nothing like
the dusting of snow on the frozen
lawn out front
or the evergreens
muffling the traffic on Albert Street).

Patrons squint into cases to see
how it's made: *Mére* and *Groszmama*, the flesh
of an elegy to Time and the Shopkeep.
The sculptor's father leans
from a spindle-back chair (how he
listens — for you are the guest).
A window opens for the mind's egress.
Bruce settles into his dream,
noses up to the fence

back in Pense, and shrugs the way a bull does,
a muscular thought surfacing: then the whole body leans —
a continent of drift. Sun bleaches grass. Everything resists.
The blue air beats: *This. And this alone.*

In the field by his shop, the sculptor
talks to the creatures he knows, the menagerie
he can't sell or hasn't the heart to let go. There
in the starlight, there without judgement.
No one to whisper, *Children, don't touch.*

THE SAME LIGHT

At two thousand feet above sea level
it's the same light everywhere. The roseate
light of September soaks through the stubble on the edge of town

and it's the same light that pools between mountains
in the rye fields of Peru, though they call it winter,
not autumn.

The grey mist of Halifax lives
in the Lima rain that has refused to fall for three hundred years.
Promises, promises.

Before the day's heat, bolting galvanized grain bins together,
I've been laid out flat by a cold sip of water. One farmer
died that day, his tractor kept turning circles in the field

until his son found him. It's the blaze and the maw,
the same jar of water that throbs in its place in the slag and dirt
on the floor of a foundry in a suburb of Prague.

Hear the wailing, the dubious appeal of the wronged.
When there is no one else, the damned curse the damned,
and that language too is known. Grief whispers to all.

LIFE IN THE CANOPY

Strolling home, I linger by the boulevard — waist-high lilies
spilling from the places where I learned
to speak and climbed each spring into the canopy
as Gaelic trees recalled the valleys of their tongues.

I resolved to live one whole year
in the creaking chevrons of their branches,
my battered lunch box lowered down with string,
balogna sandwiches going up with piping hot
sealer jars of tea, stuffed in winter socks to keep them warm.

My silver dog slept in the sun on the south side of the tree,
waiting for something buttered to fall from the airy bakeries of Heaven.

I wouldn't come down when old Walter wandered the map of the lane,
poking into garbage cans — a habit
his scavenging brain couldn't shake after the war. Mrs. Walter
finally went searching: *Walter, Walter.* And it fell to me to keep track
of the old man's coming and going. I was a puzzle to Walter,
who cocked his head like a bird to get a better look: a boy in a tree

for a reason he thought he knew but couldn't remember
and was too embarrassed to ask.
>*Hello Walter.*
>*Hello Boy.*

I wouldn't come down in spite of the shadows of things, the greening.
My hammock swayed with the branches and I was taken for shade.
I mocked the crows as they mocked me, and as I was big
and wingless we called it a draw.

Challenge songs of robins hurled themselves like javelins —
a trajectory of close escapes, cats on roofs
and flimflam lightning rods. Grooved rain
whirled down the corner spouts of the doctor's house,
splattering stacks of terra cotta pots inverted
like a ziggurat: Babylon in every garden.

The last song vanished in the magic hour.
South of town, a Rembrandt moon
paused above the Riverside cenotaph:
     kenos taphos, the empty tomb —
no river either, only rows
of stones echoing stones, abbreviated names
glistening modestly in a night without frost.
In their driven lives, the men beneath them
could never atone for having been delivered.
Released at last, they return to their ranks
and draw lots by the Moro, the Scheldt. The seasick stoker,
gone to meet the ones who died.

The tumbling moon became a Ferris wheel,
a zinc-white wagon wheel tracing figure-eights
in the arena as high-stepping heavy horses
shook their ribbonned manes as if to say,
consider these infinities:
   Birch Basket.
     Beaded Fine Bag.

The winners of the 1927 Indian Fair announced:
Jennie Dion, Mary Jane Bear, Frank Spotted Ball.
The *Exhibition News* in full.

Trains eased by the crumbling roundhouse:
a roofless coliseum, the maze of pits filled in
and the galleys gone. In columns under tels, welders
tip their masks ready to flip the window closed — the brief
moment of blindness when one darkness
becomes another from which everything's born
in a blue-white lotus of fire.

Wild swans crossed the night, calling softly
in their staggered lines,
the earthen brow below — a few pale notes
the stars guide south. Who are we
to refuse such things the privilege of being heard,
their place among the murmurs of the canopy.
There was no need to ask.
I would not come down.

ON A CLEAR DAY YOU CAN SEE FOREVER

My son is bald. A week ago his reddish-blond curls
swept his shoulders. Now he looks like King Tut.
And I have to admire the way he just did it, no discussion,
to raise some funds for cancer research — a scheme
dreamed up by the kids at school.
The problem is that now he can plainly see
his receding hairline.
"Bummer,"
he says, as he studies the two beaming peninsulas
reaching back from his temples.
Somehow
my hair,
which has grown white
since he came along,
isn't an issue. I used to do
two hundred sit-ups without breaking a sweat.
Now all that tone
has turned to the same modest pot
my father had. The good news is
I can give up trying. No more
jumping out of the hot tub

for a roll in the snow to get a rise from the kids.
No more, "Go ahead, crank 'er up," when *Radio Head* comes on.
For the rest of the year the kid will be looking up
shampoo facts
and seven dietary tips for healthy follicles. I assure him
it's simply a case of unlucky genes, his mother's:
just one more gift
from his family he did nothing to earn. And now
that he knows, he won't have a chance
to enjoy his own vanity.
Welcome to Adultsville, Daddy-o.

INTERVIEW

I went to his school today, dreading it
as usual and it came down to me
and the parents of another kid I'll never know,
talking to the home room teacher
exactly the way I'm talking to you now,

and the father starts to speak plainly
about how he can't take it when his daughter's practice
runs past five — just about when his chemo
kicks in, terminal cancer of some kind.
All of us certain of it, him for sure.

You can't give up, you know how it is —
maybe that's not exactly what he said but it's
the truth, and the teacher said how
on the farm her mother kept her cancer
from the girls for three months
until after they were gone to the States,
to university or wherever it is children go.

Clear thinking, a choice like that, but it becomes
a weight afterward.

We hardly talked about our kids; it didn't matter.
The absence in the room wasn't theirs anyway.
The buzzer signalled time to leave.
We could have stayed but didn't. We waited
as the teacher shut the door and the four of us
moved away in silence.

DRUM VILLAGE *Ness Creek, Saskatchewan*

You steal away
                           as families sleep.
              Drums in the rain.
They go all night no matter what, like a story
with a life of its own, the way a heart goes on beating no matter
how many times the song says it's been broken or stolen,
or it sways when the loved one speaks, or it's closed or open,
and stitched together like a beggar's shirt.

The way they keep at is so much like you, a natural
for all your resistance: the way you teach
a child how a drum
                    speaks muscle and skin,
the deep vocabulary of your patience.

It's like those college classes where they teach all those stressed
and sleepless students to relax as it's explained
that the person who swears they can't be hypnotized
makes the best subject because resistance is also
a kind of attention.

Rain pocks the tent and the drops stay.
Rain on skin. Perhaps the first drum.
                            I fall asleep listening.
Just last week the song
                lost for years in the flute
I bought in Peru rose through the house like a strange grey bird.
That too was you; a kind of grace,
                the way love, without trying,
humbles our intentions.

ELSA'S ARGYLE STREET SERENADE

That writer next door. Don't they know
an old person needs to sleep. It's bad enough
I have to get up at four every morning
to pee and have a cigarette
then get up at seven to pour nicotine water
on the slugs before they get to the tomatoes,
but Lord, don't they have enough sense to close their windows
when they're going at it? The first time it happened I thought
someone was being murdered, and almost called
the police. It isn't that I haven't been around
the block, my love, because I have, Oh yes, but it isn't
a contest. Not that they aren't nice people,
better than the last lot. That smell coming out of there
sure wasn't tea leaves — people coming all hours of the night
and sometimes they got the house wrong
and came to my place and kept banging away
until I got up. I should have told them to go to hell
but I'm not naïve. These kids I don't mind.
But close the damn window.

And Alice over here —
crazy as a bag of hammers. She runs up
to the fence and yaps about my spruce
dropping needles in her yard and shading
her wormy lettuce. She wants me to chop it down.
Sixty-foot of tree. What should I use, a hatchet?
What an embarrassment. Maybe if it landed on her house
it would knock some sense into her.
It was that husband of hers, the way
that bastard knocked her around.
Never said two words, and that's always a sign. It was always
his friends, she said once, never hers.
Not before he died and not after.
She complains about my tree instead.
She starts right in, so I light up a cigarette, which she hates,
and I put the butt in my nicotine water, which she tells me
disgusts her, and to make her point
she starts beating at her potato hills with a hoe. You'd think
she'd let them keep their heads if they want to. Shoot me
and take me away in a barrow
if I get like that. Natter-brained
coots like her give old folks a bad name.

ELSA'S DREAM

March and the chorus of hundreds of waxwings
moves up the street, the racket comes in
through the chinks where putty has fallen away from the window
and the panes tremble. Elsa dreams of the puffins

back home, streaking out from crevasses in dark cliffs,
the sudden burring of sharp wings
plunging into the whitecaps and coming out with beaks
full of flapping capelin. Her brother Paul smiles

in his green boots and pullover, seventeen years old
as he stands below her. Moving gear to the middle
of the dory, he lays a gaff on the net he uses
for herring when he goes after baitfish.

She nods as he speaks. Elsa can't hear what he says
but she understands. A wave surges up from a thin arm of rock
in the harbour. She can't hold on to his voice but she knows
how it feels. The harder the land, the softer we speak.

The waxwings move again, a sliding that sharpens the edge
of the air. The sealing boat heaves in a sea the colour
of old stones, and Elsa sees Paul in the crowsnest, mitts
wrapped 'round the mast.

Captain's ordered him up two hours ago because
he's the youngest, but nobody's checked. He bends toward the bow
like he's part of the boat. A mask of sea ice covers his face
and the deep age in his open eyes.

Elsa speaks and people can't tell where
she's from anymore. Sometimes she meets a missus
who lived up the shore and they always rehearse
the endless lists of each other's people. There are things

that mustn't be spoken because it's bad luck. The houses
hold on to the slope going down to the bay and the women
are used to looking out over anxious water empty of boats.
And just like the men, they learn to take it.

COYOTE WILLOW *Salix exigua*

In the city core, where there are no native trees,
the coyote willow leans out from an earthen dike —
a volunteer refusing to be cleared off like a weed by the City crew.
We're drylanders here and know the value
of a tree, as if the King's broad-arrow were
carved in the trunk,
halfway round the side where it says
                                  Tomas ♡ Renée.
This morning in the café, light pooled in the new plate before me,
a shadow, a shoreline, then the Willow formed,
the tale told in the Buddha's time: two lovers
pursued over a bridge by the father and a jilted suitor,
sometimes with three figures, sometimes with four.
The father follows their boat to an island and sets fire
to the hut where the lovers are sleeping.
                              There is a word for this kind of murder,
an old one, but the willow by the creek knows more of the fish
nudging the wall of the weir under the bridge
than it does about genius, impeccable cobalt glaze,
or the thousand poor copies of Thomas Minton's design.

Sandbar willow, narrow-leaf, slender willow — they're all
the same thing, which only goes to show what a chameleon
it is. Crying tree, daughter of Esos from which stabbed men
bleed as they hang, winter harp, moon-tree, healer,
river-rooted, vernal, sign post and eye, death-pillow, bed:
                                                unweave yourself;
let others be swayed by varnished landscapes
with elegiac cattle milling about like death-in-the-background.
Bend into this failing river, this want
                                 of water, re-
choir your names
                        Coyōte
                                Coyōtee   *Coyōtay.*
                                             Willow.

MY SO-CALLED CAREER

could have been better, but hasn't been bad.
Though I did save someone once, or I think I did.
There's no point trying to measure a night like that.
The girl in the dark saying softly, "I was just
thinking of jumping off the bridge."

I found her waiting in that White Cross
kitchen — for what, she wouldn't say.
I may never be better than I was in those four hours.

It's like the photographer who stops, *Saigon 1973*,
as he hurries to the briefing — a baby
in a cardboard box,
her brother curled beside her, asleep
as the world walks by them.
But the picture goes out on the wire
and the world does look: she's flown to the States
where a heart operation
saves her life, and she stays
and grows up. Think what that's like
when you know she lives,

almost your own,
as if you had washed her hair,
got her teeth fixed and made sure
she wore braces, and you paced in Emergency,
no messing around as her fever kept going up and she couldn't
swallow, and her head ached, and she wept
as politely as she could while the doctors made up their minds,
and you wondered: *Is this me in this room all day and all night,*
getting the nurse, getting the doctor, cooling her face
with a cloth, uselessly wishing her pain into me?
The girl in the box had no say.
It would have been easy.
Simple for some — to leave her.

But the *action* is there, inside you:
indelible — in the place
you thought you were saving
for the birth of a child;
and its voice in you whispers, *It is.*
It is.

HEART

Heart
          is the weem where we sleep
just beyond reason,
                where truth is admitted
and betrayal stares out
from a crate we have opened
                            many times.

It is the place where we speak
                        when we have nothing left,
where the poet says, *Come,*
          sit down inside me.

It used to be thought that the heart resides
in the stomach,

which is why it is still the custom
to say "Our hearts in our throats."

                                        And if not
for the grim exactitude of men with lamps,
some merely curious,
                        crowding round a half-draped cadaver,
we would still need a place on the left side,
just off the breastbone,

where sorrows flow
                and without which
we would rise every morning and walk through the world

with a pauper's death in our eyes.

ME AND DAD AT THE REGINA RIOT *June 30, 1933*

"You try too hard," my father says.
And he tips the brim of his new fedora —
a bit of a dandy for a minister's son.
He's seventeen, which is young for a ghost,
but you know my father.

Tear gas. We stand on 11th and Osler,
eyes streaming. A wall of police, hell-bent
on black horses
                    charge down the sidewalk.
We back into a doorway. A squad down the side street,
waiting in ambush. "So much
for the salt of the earth," says my dad.

                    I take out
                              my notebook: *Fighting in all
                                        directions. Old man
            with face split open taken to police garage.*

"Put that away," Dad says.
And he's right.
His eyes are grey. Grey sky, grey water.

A detective lies with his head caved in. Al Hill tries to lift him.
The movie keeps rolling. My father knows death.
No one can stop it.

❧

The Olympia Café — still selling sandwiches. Jack Brenner slumps on a stool —
      two black eyes.

He holds his head between his hands, squeezes
the lights in his brain to make them stop, says to someone I can't see,
         "Just wherever they could, they
hit him... they were hitting him on the head and wherever
they could — arms and everything. He was
      smothered in blood. You couldn't
see who he was, you could see
      he was a man, and I saw
one that I know, Sergeant Terry Logan, and I said, *What are you
trying to do, are you*
      trying to kill him?"

❧

The Mounties shoot into groups, shooting low.
                                  The order from Bennett: *Stop them here —*
               I don't care how.

The strikers form ranks of four,
               march back to their tents out by the stadium.
A necklace of Mounties with .303s
to keep them there. A few start to sing,
Hold the fort for we are coming...
               but they can't keep it up.

Three men pass by. The one in the middle
half-staggers.
               A crust of blood stiffens his shirt.
My father wants to go with them. It must be the soldier
in him, the part that has seen the meaning
of "the bitter end."

There are things you face. They change you
or they become an addiction. I have seen my father
in Italy under camouflage netting after Monte Casino,
						writing letters
to families, to wives if married, to mothers if single,
a field full of coffins on the way up the line,
gone the first morning.

			There's a picture I keep in my office:
an unnamed poet recites in Arabic from a platform of rubble,
balanced there like the well-mannered ghost of starvation.
The photographer sees all the righteous and dirty
Disasters of War, but no one has told him Goya
is dead.

Mayor Cornelius Rink pulls up to the stadium gate.
Jumps out of the car and stamps his feet. "You communist
sons of bitches. You made this wreck. Who's going to pay?
You goddamn asses?"

"Send it to Bennett," my father replies.
An echo comes back from the armoury wall. Rink stops.
"Send that bastard the bill."

MIRA, WITH BLACK GUITAR

                    You play your black guitar. The notes
escape through the open window and hang like velvet pairs

                                    in the sway of the darkness.

A lamp spills over the room

you've arranged for yourself.
                            A young woman's clothes.

You never did go for teen magazines:
                    how little I know. Even so,

the page is still open, and whatever they say,
                          time's not against us.

Trees arch over the street. Beneath the eclipse of a stop sign
the sidewalk appears,

                      dappled in moonlight.

                                            Air feels its way over the sill.

You stand with a dancer's sense of space,
                    the instrument shut in its case

                          with the questions
that were never meant to have answers.

REGINA CONSERVATORY

Mothers wait for their daughters
dancing in black one floor above

while a man with his son waits
in the hall round the corner, the no-go zone.

The mothers are busy with all the minutiae, the thousand
invisible duties that baffle the man.

If you ask he will tell you he no longer thinks of the future.
If work is the life raft the life raft is sinking.

With quick, light strokes of a day-glow pen, one of the mothers
illuminates the text from a night course, *Accounting and Time*.

In movement above, slendering flowers
sway in the clearing

and raise their pale arms as Mistress explains that the swans
were not really swans.

LAST NIGHT

Last night I slept in the Nesbitt Forest,
dreaming the town I grew up in.

I speed over darkness, looking away.
                              This must be flying.

Life-sized wooden people have been placed on the boardwalk:
blonde cowboys on rearing palominos, women strolling —
figures my uncle carves then gives away.
                          All of them live.
All of them know me.

Light becomes the hour it owns.
                              Dawn arrives.
Dreams are supposed to lead somewhere,
but this one leads back to itself, like a forest
or the trickle that seeps through the sand under the trailor, going deeper,
                    wrapping itself around the roots of trees weakened with iron rot —
a system of capillaries that pushes rocks upward for no end.

I once filled a crow full of arrows and it wouldn't die.
I almost drowned once, but I don't remember.
I got lost in a place full of sink-holes, but just walked out.
Who were those people alive in their wood?
                    From the day I was born
my fear was profound for all the right reasons.

A WINDOW

It's hard to get used
to the place you saw in your mind
before you built it.

Acts of faith
will be required.
The setting sun
will keep its place
if you stay.

Fringes of cloud
candesce like strands of heated wire
against the purple sky. You're sure
you passed through them
as you drove toward hills,
before they vanished:
a mantle in darkness.
Now you pass though them again.

And though you work late
you have yet to describe
the belligerent elm,
its tapping half-severed,
branches probing until nighttime scrapes
become syllables of sleep and you lie there exhausted,
dreaming
in another language, part of you
wanting it to stop as something else whispers,
Go ahead. Open me.

WALKING

Twilight enters the place where things have been and the ordinary gap
        where there is nothing to embrace. Light withdraws
between the bungalows, its alibis full of fences and the tinkle of a lady's bracelet.

These are the settled nights of June, loved as they were when I walked
        with my father, his stories going back and back to evenings.
His voice is sometimes gone, or maybe it's still here, choosing to be silent.

We have grown to sound alike and it feels like theft to think of his voice then,
        when it was full of something to be told — not a marvel,
but a vast array of details viewed obliquely, like the skin of a young canoe,

when the craftsman's light comes in from the side and a tough hand strokes
        the ripples in the ash and the thing being made
is admired for what it has not yet become.

And there I was in that northern town that had not yet chosen
        between the civilized south and wilderness, the unreadable river
half a mile wide and filled with fish as cold and elusive as the moon.

We strolled past neighbours' newly seeded lawns as the last heat surged, the exhausted air,
        cool at last as violet fringed the crowns of new trees
still tied to their stakes with ribbons as if they were not yet old enough to leave.

The two of us moved to the gait of my father's voice. Sometimes I was the one who asked
        after supper if he wanted to go for a walk, knowing he would come.
For my father, then, there was always some story.

It took years to hear them all. When I did it felt like a kind of death, but not then —
        then, I knew: to speak is to walk, and I, the silent son, the one who hardly spoke,
felt that I, too, in turn had spoken.

AS HE LEFT ME

I knew when I got the call, hurried four blocks
to his house in the dark,
shouldered the bathroom door open,
busting the lock. The weight
on the other side was his weight:
my father dead. Then my brother came in.

The 911 operator was
talking me through mouth-to-mouth
as my brother knelt, heel of one hand
over the other, pushing expertly
on my father's chest, both of us calm
through the required motions,
the obligations
of the last one to feel his warmth leave.

I was glad for the decision
that would no longer have to be made,
for him and for me. The EMT confirmed
what everyone knew — there was no emergency.

The police asked: *Was he sick? What time
did this happen? Was it 2:00 a.m.?
4:00 a.m.?* Hell,
I didn't know.
The Coroner asked too: *Who is his doctor?*
And my mother made tea because people might want some tea,
and she answered precisely
the questions nobody asked: it happened
at last and that was all there was to it.

I left the room, went upstairs to close his eyes
and felt how cool he suddenly was. I said a few words
about the trick he played on us all. The silence
was warm and right, not bitter as it could have been.
I felt the lightness
of things, how little matters, and though in our lives
we never embraced,
an hour before I didn't even think
of my mouth on his as I watched his chest rise
then fall, futile and strange.
The breath of the dead.

APPETITE

I sometimes think the only reason I've become
the family cook is that Mother was a hard-core Scot.
The only things she could truly cook
were turkey and Nanaimo bars.

And so today I barbequed swordfish, splashed
Point Pelee wine
into lightly searing scallops and felt like a fraud: some foods
cook themselves. The spices are superfluous.
Lobster drenched in heated garlic butter: what could be simpler?
Yet anytime I make chowder
I think of my sister, the two of us
a thousand miles from home
and the sweet smells
filling the drafty kitchen,
oven door propped shut, gingery
war cake, so-called because it cures for a week and makes good eating
weeks after that.

I still long for anything tasting of the sea, the necessity
of the food of the sea, and things that last.
Now I cook poor man's food for family gatherings: baked mackerel
and *Bruce's Special,* exotic because it is strange

out here in the West and because they imagine my adventures, a life
so surely different than their own. For my part I enjoy
a crowded table, something savoured,
the way wheels of light rock and scatter
in a conversation, the same voices
and the same light years from now.

I was not burdened in my absence, ten years
of missed Thanksgivings, Mother up all night, basting
the browning fowl and drinking Glenfiddich doubles,
water on the side. It was easy leaving;
easy coming home.

My sister says I learned my gypsy ways too young
and now I have an orphan's appetite for everything.
Each new dish I loved tasted like another home.
But now we're orphans, truly — parents gone.
And so we make ourselves again. Who can fill such spaces?
Table set, I return the jar of tarragon.
The muted dust of spice invades the cupboard
and everyone is waiting,
lost before the legend of all that we've consumed.

FLYWAY

Birds never stay long in a northern refuge.
They are merely
                    passing through.
Twice a year life gathers and the air applauds.

In these days of disappearance
it is fortunate to be
                        a stretch of weedy lake
dropping from a rim of untilled prairie,

the shuffling tongues of last year's shoregrass
waiting for the green   *as if.*

Two miles out a shadow
stirs the plain; a thousand Arctic swans form like rain,
come in through fallow light, taken into gravity

as it draws their calling home — to a refuge
they never asked for, and so, is ours.

VACANCY *Prince Albert National Park, Saskatchewan*

There's nothing so desolate as a campsite after the tent
has been struck and the packed gravel
leaves no explanation or name.
Gone is the appetite that, hours ago, dark had for fire;
the hiss of the Coleman snuffed out.

Gone is the soft infusion of potatoes and onion
sizzling in olive oil and the blood innuendo of browning meat.
Gone is the invisibility dark bestows,
the possibilities that tremble like aspen leaves,
when all the instruments of time have stopped
and memory overflows its banks and residues
rise from the silt where they've slept all along.

Light stops for surfaces, the inexplicable scabs
of the present for which permits are required
and check-out time is always too early.
So back slowly away, leave an elegy to emptiness,
to absent friends and the wounded who summoned you,
with whom you spoke until they were done speaking
in the endless hour after midnight.

WASKESIU *Prince Albert National Park, Saskatchewan*

On line 107 of a poem about ravens
spindly black poplars are shouldered aside
                              by spruce on their home ground.
Seedlings battle
        like baby sharks in the clearing where sun punches through
to the undergrowth.

                        The Canadian Shield swells like a reef
as God stakes down the four corners of the park
and unrolls the camping gear.
                                    It's one of the places
He didn't want to let go of, although in the fine print
He let Parks Canada put in a road.

The next eight cantos go on to say
                there is something in us
that glows through and through like stones in a hard sweat.
It cracks through to the heart if dropped
        and you can find those cold half-shells of granite
on the shore above the waterline.
                            Their razor edge is the reason
        red deer walk lightly,
the way people step between graves.

         And somewhere it says that daylight is shallow,
with stars just behind it and it drops off
like a dangerous lake where you swim
               at your own risk.
You take it for granted the polestar
will keep things in place.
                                      You sleep
on a mattress of your own breath and it's obvious:
Heaven is full of things.
                       We put telescopes on mountains
and send them into space where they tell us
there is more and more we can't see.

Old Raven turns up
like a peninsula of blood at a kill site.
         New Raven is a slurry of rotten snow
and usually ends in an interrogative:
Let's go to the dump, eh?

We're told there's no word for dump in Old Raven.
Just the lake curving high,
                          only lake on the horizon as you hop
from bone to bone and make jokes with the wolf
that starved by the shoreline.
Now all it can do is grin.

NOT ZEN BUT CLOSE ENOUGH *Elk Island National Park, Alberta*

The axe, seized in wet wood, its chill,
a heart-groan travelling downward.
Blue buds of flame make a ring in the ticking Coleman.

The tents in this old park nudge each other
like grandchildren at a reunion. Too close
and too familiar, their attention turns inward.

The rain holds off for hours, falling and not falling
like the pause after the toll of a bell. Poplars hiss, a failed
and restless meditation. Better to intend nothing.

The clanking bulldozer levels the beach.
The squirrel breaks into a pack of instant porridge
it drags across the table. In woods beyond,

ragged beards stroke the ground
as black bodies of solitary bison, heads down,
nuzzle the grass. Their small, weak eyes see

what they need to see. They are neither
quick nor slow. Summer's dark beast, birth-mark in snow.
The sign on the gate warns:

Do not approach them; they are here
on the shore of the present.
That is enough.

INSIDE THE QUALITY TEA ROOM

                    regulars come in from the crisp morning air and the weekend, peer past
the tops of eye-level curtains as a vapour trail quickens the sky, an inkling
of frost in the air — but it's September isn't it? —

as the waitress pours coffee into bottomless cups of second-shift customers, her white slacks from
Zellers picking up smoke and the smell of the kitchen.

❧

      A half lemon pie shines out from its shelf. Two native silk screens
      dream up a past on a peach-coloured wall.

      There are three wide-angle prints of Regina, horizons stacking one above the other like
            upside-down saucers as they make their mental exits left
      and right of the frame.

      In the picture on top Percherons wait. Air rolls over their necks in a wave. Their steady
            bodies: a prize team of perfectly repeating forms at the side
               of a trainless station.

❧

In pictures below, the town's been made over the way the Quality Tea Room's been made over from corner store and coffee bar,

a top-loaded cooler humming away like a red vault in a victory fortress of canned food and Brillo Pads until the owner and the wire windings of the motor
gave way to old age, the buck

        sky-rocket inflation
             the kids
       the car
    the Hearing Aid Plan
          confused socialism

  and anti-smoking bylaw color theory decor.

There's a Spanish courtyard where inserted birch trees grow up toward
a square blue hole.

Their skins are as pale as the Czarina's children and they
appear to be dying

                              of too much shade, who they are
                    and other romantic diseases.

But inside the Quality Tea Room plates clatter. Bored kids scuff their feet
        in time on the floor as they hunch over tables,
chins on their hands and sound games going on in the backs of their mouths

              Ladder ladder ladder Stop that.

                 Ladder ladder

      Stop. That. In this day
after Labor Day cafe where regulars talk Roughriders.

           One of the boys
wears a green and white hat that says *Leask, Saskatchewan*. The Safeway meat manager
perched at the counter pours over his paper,
                              opens it so,
     putting finger to thumb with Buddha-like flare.

At quarter past ten the backlit arm of the Co-op clock swings round to a grazing herd
of Pythagorean cows.

                One of them raises her head, right ear cocked
as she listens to the music of the neighbourhood.
                          She dreams she lives under a cork tree

where bands of Moorish gypsies strum their blue guitars
        and pass through tragic landscapes on their journey into exile.
                Then morning swirls in like a dime-a-dance girl and glides to her seat,
     taking some refuge

and maybe some tea. No need to ask if she's been here before. She just looks in
                                    your cup,
    stirring the leaves.

Pools of violet light drain from the nineteen-cent vases;
the confessional of the coffee booth gives way to dissolving chains of connection.

A man slides to his seat in his perfect Valentino, his monogrammed
handkerchief D.H.T. with the letters *D* and *H*
                                        pressed to his lips.

There's a change in the music, a complex Segovian
                beat of invisible fingers

                            tapping on panes.

                    Inside the Quality Tea Room
the smells and the colors go on

in a rain that has lasted for years.

PLOUGH WINDS

I sleep with the Zuck boys, Gary and Dale, in the loft of a cattle barn that's lain
                                                                                                      empty for years.
We wake up on remnants of hay we hauled up the ladder —
our sleeping bags, thin as cheesecloth, little more than sacks
                                                                                             and lumpy clots of batting.
                                                 The cold
August night is still trapped in the rafters. We shiver as wind rattles the slats
in the ventilator shafts above us, a surge in the air. Then rain
                          explodes
without warning, as if nails being dropped from a great height are rolling
down the roof.

The loft door bangs open, pinned to the side of the barn as the wind
          drives bullets
of water into slaked wood. Small stones picked up in the yard whiz past our ears like
                                         shrapnel.
The three of us twist back into the darkness trapped in the barn.

We're in love with the wind, the way that its voices tumble like stones.
We string ourselves out along hilltops, spread our arms like the masts
of radio receivers as we wait for the whispers, the language
of wire, the boom of a sail. Our ten-gun brig
sends lines to the depths in search of our origins.
Black clouds give birth to lightning as birds
fall exhausted out of the sky. We wait for the flood
and the end of the flood; seventeen hundred and forty-two days at sea,
when the journey will end and the habitable world
is once more our home.

A burst of hail wallops the ground and the house,
                                          hammers
the tin roof of the machine shed
and the rusty cattle trough. Chickens fight for a place in the cast iron
stove that walked away from the summer kitchen twenty years ago. The barn takes the
                                                            beating.

We shout to each other. Gary's not sure the roof will hold up. Muddy streams braid into rivers that rush down the hill, flooding the barn. Floorboards
                                                                               shake.
Joists shift and creek,
                the rising thrum —
joined by banging in the empty stalls. Something is trying to kick its way free.

                Five horses vanish. Perhaps they knew — took the way through the gap
                and into the hills. They've abandoned their silver,
                their saddles inlaid with opening roses and lapis from stirrup to cantle.
                They are gone into the blue walls of Nineveh Gate
                and the walls of burial rooms. They leave by the desert
                or by way of the plain. Escaparé:
                they escaped or were stolen, painted ochre on skin — a horse dance,
                a rattle. They've gone into smoke, the cascading sparks of steel wheels sliding on steel as
                fingers of grassfire peel at the skin of screaming soil.

                Strings of dust sift from the roof of the stable.
                The skull by the door grins its last grin
                and makes ready to crumble. The main beams shriek
                but there's no one to hear or carry to Caesar news of the downfall.

We skip four rungs of the ladder and jump to the ground. The stable is halfway
to the house and we run for it: two log walls on the windward side;
                              the rest is open.

We leap from one patch of chickweed to another, slipping in greasy mud.
My head and shoulders feel like they're being pounded by sticks.
                The stable's a blur.
Gary's mom is waving from the porch.

>   *We race to the door where she waits*
>   *with raven hair and her vanishing act.*
>   *The house disappears, leaves only a frame.*
>   *Walls turn into windows.*
>   *Flowers lie down in the field of her dress*
>   *and she seems to be asking: Why, why*
>   *are we running? A flock of sheltering birds*
>   *explodes from the grass and it's*
>   *snatched away sideways. Oh, she says. Oh.*

A blue-white crust of hail covers the ground, cool as the sheet on the face of a corpse.
                Windows
                              gape in the barn.

The storm's opaque curtain grazes the crest of the field, we can't see
the farm on the southwest horizon,
                                      but we think it's still there.
        The hail
turns to rain. A sheet of plywood lifts off the ground, cartwheels across the yard,
                                    snags in the poplars,
and delivers itself to the trees it came from like a manila envelope marked *Return to Sender.*

The stable shrieks and the two walls fly straight out as if they're on hinges.
                            The rickety hulk floats on a cushion of air
then the whole thing crashes down and detonates into splinters.
We stare at the place where we should have been standing.

                We turn away: we abandon; pale
                            battered roses cling to the ditch.

            The sky is an echo no more — summer's long vale drifting empty.
                    Gone, our swift harbour.

                                        Mr. Zuck swore
he was done. He traded the farm for a bungalow in town, a place
with running water and bedrooms for the kids.

                                        The developer stripped
the home quarter for topsoil and flattened the house.

The town annexed the land to make room for a hospital and subdivisions
                              with cul-de-sacs and split-level houses.

On the day of the plough wind we had no way to know that the stable was already
a point on a map, its fate sealed months before.
                                        Those kinds of maps
come in layers with buffers for aquifers and trunk lines worked out by ratios,

                                        They are mostly ideas
with densities for schools, imagined futures with elevations sent in by satellite.
Willow bluffs circle the sloughs like a cartoon oasis — no one's loss,
                                        the surface

scraped clean
                           and the past erased with no regard

for answerless questions: why we were spared, or how we
                         escaped

the wind's lament and its outrage.

SASKATOON BERRY

My tall cousin is more elegant
than I am; both of us
poets — and some local kitchen god
brings us to adjacent tables at a conference in Moose Jaw.

If a small tornado
were to set down on this pleasant deck,
half the poets in Saskatchewan would be swept away
with the doilies. I order Saskatoon *pie à la mode*
and the poets at my table discuss
the commercial version of the purple berry, how the growers
water less, which produces a smaller berry
and concentrates the sugar. They're called
service berries in Ontario and Indian berries in Nova
Scotia but it seems they're only eaten seriously
in the West. Folks here say they're better
than the blue berry, which grows up North,
or the legendary
appleberry of Newfoundland and Labrador.
But this is where we are and what we eat.

I picked my first Saskatoons by my grandfather's cabin. Pulled
fat berries, red and purple, from tall bushes — the forest
full of eyes; and we were always careful
about the black bear sow.
There are many tales of berry pickers
startled from a nap by the grunt of a bear pulling stems to the ground
on the other side of the bush and it always
ends the same way: backing away from a pail brimming
with berries or the howl of a toddler that sends the bear wheeling one way
and kids scrambling another.

But the point is the berries.
Pie browning in a woodstove
on a ninety-two degree July afternoon, the stove
overheating the cabin and the fruity lava
bubbling over and forming fresh caps on the mountain range
of black scars on the bottom of the oven, two pies
gone in a sitting and a little left over to cool until evening
when the minty scent of spruce edges up against
the terracotta glow of the cabin and mosquitoes
warm up their singing voices between the glass and the curtains.

Every place has its simple foods, a gesture
toward the place itself. Something to do
with the way we speak when we speak of things
only our people would know: the warm rush
of air driven high in the aspens
before there is rain; how fireweed
lives by the road — a summer of dust; or wilderness,
if only we love it enough.

SWANS

Mira opens the lacquered wings of her vanity,
then brushes her hair. She's bussing tables at 4:00.
Keegan's down in the studio, making plans on his cell
as he paints with one hand. This is the end of April
and the swans on Long Lake are getting ready to fly, a *V*
that glides easily over last year's fields.
This is the third year I've missed seeing them go,
taking turns in the lead as their turbulence
moves down the line: lift for following wings.

My kids want to move to exotic B.C. —
Keegan, to follow his musical friends.
Mira is waiting for winter and the ski trip
to Kimberly, to carve down the slopes
until she's exhausted.
I was born in the mountains but I'll never go.

Keegan talks faster — some new idea starting to fly.
Mira is all business now. She heads downstairs,
clothes in her bag, but she stops.
Turning toward me, she holds up her hand
like a mask, then pulls it away to show me
her "server's face." Then she laughs.

It's a mystery to me where they get this stuff:
things I never did; some I've forgotten.
The two of them getting ready to leave
just as I'm coming home.

AUTHOR'S NOTES

Winter. The quote is from Archibald Lampman's (1861-1899) famous poem celebrating Canadian winters, "January Morning."

The Wind. The Regina cyclone swept through Regina on Sunday, June 30, 1912 as residents prepared for Dominion Day. The cyclone started south of town and swept through the business district. The final death toll was 28. The Province and Federal Governments provided no help. It took the City 40 years to pay off the loan from the Province to cover the damage.

Dear Bob, Your Smallpox Blanket. Bob Boyer (1948-2004), a Métis artist born near Prince Albert, Saskatchewan created a series of maps and small pox blankets in a reclaiming of Métis and First Nation history.

A New Manifesto. The Regina Manifesto of 1933 was adopted at the July meeting of the first national conference of the Canadian Commonwealth Federation (CCF). The manifesto is a watershed of modern social policy. It called for a planned economy and a rational approach to social policy, marketing boards and scientifically-based agriculture, unemployment insurance, government-owed utilities and control of communications and transportation, government insurance, Medicare, the removal of immigration barriers, the establishment of cooperatives, and strong basic freedoms based on the hard lessons of the '30s. The New Manifesto draws on the language and imagery of the original.

My So-Called Career. The poem is inspired by the photograph, Baby in a Box, by now-retired AP photographer Charles (Chick) Harrity. As the poem indicates, public response to the photograph that went out over the wire was so great that the girl was found and brought to the United States.

Me and Dad at the Regina Riot. In 1933, Conservative Prime Minister R. B. Bennett ordered the RCMP to stop 1,000 On-to-Ottawa trekkers traveling by box car to Ottawa to protest conditions in relief camps for single men operated by the Department of National Defence. The result was a police riot in Regina on June 30, just after Trek leaders had spent a full day meeting with Saskatchewan Premier James Gardiner and his Cabinet. Panic broke out in the crowd of 1,800 when police attempted to arrest the leaders at an evening fundraising rally in Market Square. One trekker and a policeman were killed at the riot. A second trekker died of injuries later. Over 250 were injured as the battle spread though the business district. Regina writer, June Mitchell, remembers her parents hiding trekkers from the police after the riot. It was the day before Dominion Day, and 23 years to the day of the Regina Cyclone of 1912. The poem is informed by Bill Waiser's book, *All Hell Can't Stop Us: The On-to-Ottawa Trek and the Regina Riot*, and newspaper accounts. The liberties are mine.

Dead Métis at Batoche. Sculpture of a dead Métis by artist, Joe Fafard. The sculpture is based on a photograph of a man was killed at Batoche, Saskatchewan in 1885, the battle that ended the North West Rebellion led by Louis Riel. There is some speculation based on the amount of blood on his shirt, that the man was dragged. He lies in a pieta position with his jacket half off. The bell in the church where the Métis held out was taken as a trophy by the Canadian Army. It was stolen from the Royal Canadian Legion Hall in Millbrook, Ontario, a few days after some Métis leaders had their photograph taken in front of it. It has not been seen since. The poem was commissioned for the opening of Fafard's (2008-2009) retrospective.

Willow. The poem is inspired by the Wascana Creek willow, which the City was going to cut down to prevent erosion of the dike. The willow was saved by the protests of residents and the new design for the dike included a plan to naturalize the habitat along the creek. The willow is still there, living up to its coyote/trickster name.

AFTERWARD *Bruce Rice*

Regina will never know the totemic Douglas-fir. The urban forest we have created belongs to the human realm. Branches touch just above our heads, the canopy so close we are part of it. We have removed the rubbing stones used by bison and forgotten the now-extinct buffalo wolf. But the birds still come — kestrels, chipping sparrows, pin wheeling gulls, thrushes, waxwings, and the night migrations of September. In writing about Regina, I found myself searching for a place that is both prairie and not-prairie. My original idea was to try to write about this community as a visitor might see it — finding my own landmarks and histories. The result has turned out to be more personal — a narrative that spirals outward from my home and the block I live on.

I first met Cherie Westmoreland, whose photographs appear on the cover and between these pages, at a Saskatchewan Writers and Artists colony. Her remarkable images are imbued with the language and the emotional proximity of the almost-familiar. The original manuscript was written as a continuous text and I confess to some nervousness when the publisher suggested incorporating Cherie's photos throughout the book. It meant re-imagining the book, but the images give the motif of trees and the notion of this "human canopy" a heightened presence in the work. The result is actually closer to my original intent than the initial manuscript and I thank Cherie for her care in selecting images that expand the text and establish a true dialogue with the poems.

No one would expect to find a city here. Regina appears suddenly on the horizon. When you approach the outskirts at dawn or look in the rear view mirror as you leave in the evening, among scattered buildings, the crowns of the trees are the first and last thing light touches. Life quiets down as streetlights appear, marking the perimeter of our human islands. Cherie's photographs have taken the time to see such things and I hope these poems do too.

AFTERWARD *Cherie Westmoreland*

The conversation began with the cover image and a gathering of photographs in response to the tones, textures and terrain of Bruce's evocative manuscript. Meanings, responses, connection and interconnection took root and grew, suggesting relationships both obvious and mysterious. The fabric of words and images was being woven, emerging to surprise me with the vitality and brightness of an alive and on-going conversation.

In responding to Bruce's words and the deeply comforting and familiar sense of place that they grounded me in, the suggestion of counterpoint ran through my intuitive movement amongst my images.

I have been photographing the particular singularity of prairie trees for years. This body of work brings me down and back from the spacious expanse of prairie sky and landscape in an on-going exploration of what home place is and what it means. There is an insistent longing that argues with a reluctant rootedness in this place that continues to fuel my work.

In this particular prairie urban place where we proudly state, "And every tree is planted," we are also held and rooted by a tenacity of wild trees on the wider prairie landscape. These are trees that, in their singularity and familial groups, hold us under the larger prairie sky—threading us back into our urban home and into "the urban forest we have created"—canopies of sky and cloud and tree and human community.

Thank you, Bruce, for welcoming this connecting and continuing conversation.

ACKNOWLEDGEMENTS

The author gratefully acknowledges the support provided during the writing of this book by the Saskatchewan Arts Board, Saskatchewan Writers Guild and the SWG Writers and Artists Colony, Napa Valley Writers Conference, and members of The Poets Combine and Notes from the Underground. Support provided by Saskatchewan Arts Board and the Canada Council for the Arts for the publication of this book are also gratefully acknowledged. Finally, special thanks are due to Harold Rhenish, whose advice as editor, helped to bring it all home.